PLAYING FROM AN ORCHESTRAL SCORE

BY

ERIC TAYLOR

D1457815

MUSIC DEPARTMENT
OXFORD UNIVERSITY PRESS
44 CONDUIT STREET LONDON W.1
200 MADISON AVENUE NEW YORK N.Y. 10016

ACKNOWLEDGEMENTS are due to the following for permission to use music extracts: Boosey & Hawkes Ltd. (Britten: *Four Sea Interludes —Sunday Morning*; Finzi: *Dies Natalis—Intrada*); J. & W. Chester Ltd.(Stravinsky: *L'Oiseau de Feu*; Berkeley: *Nocturne for Orchestra*); Durand & Cie (Ravel: *Shéhérazade—I. Asie.* [piano version and score]); J. Hamelle & Cie (Fauré: *Shylock—Epithalame and Nocturne*); Alfred Lengnick & Co. Ltd. (Rubbra: *Symphony No. 5 in B flat*); Novello & Co. Ltd. (Elgar: *Wand of Youth—2nd Suite, Little Bells*); Schott & Co. Ltd. (Ravel: *Pavane pour Une Infante Défunte* [piano version and score]); Oxford University Press (Vaughan Williams: *Symphony in E Minor*).

Printed in Great Britain

PREFACE

IT MAY be a discouraging note on which to start, but the fact has to be admitted at once that a pianist cannot do justice to a work which was conceived for the orchestra. He cannot reproduce the timbres of the different instruments. He cannot sustain notes as wind and string players can, let alone shape them with a crescendo. Much of the time he cannot even play all the notes, which no doubt is one of the reasons why composers seem to prefer to arrange their works, if at all, for two players. Indeed, it would not be much of an exaggeration to say that orchestral music is effective precisely to the extent to which it can *not* be transferred to the piano.

Nevertheless, for the purposes of study, whether for one's private benefit or as a preliminary to rehearsal, the attempt to translate an orchestral work into pianistic terms is invaluable. There are those who can 'read' a score—that is, can form a mental impression of it merely by looking at it—but they are rare, and their abilities are more likely to be the result of hard work than of a charmed birth. Moreover, a sceptic might observe that the quickest way to prove the capacity to 'read' a score is to play it. 'Reading', of course, is quite different from 'following'. With the music safely going on in the background we can all persuade ourselves that the score holds no mysteries. Real 'reading', especially as tested by playing, is not at all such an easy matter. We must then *know* whether the second horn has an F♯ or an F♮, which clef the cello is in, whether the clarinets are in B♭ or A. We cannot leave it to the orchestral players to work out; the record does not go on comfortably turning.

It is because playing from an orchestral score is such a help towards a detailed and accurate understanding that most degree and some diploma examinations demand it of their candidates. Yet it is not usually an easy matter, particularly in the early stages, to find a wide enough range of suitable examples to practise, especially as miniature scores are often too small to read conveniently when placed on a piano desk. It is primarily to meet this need that the present book has been compiled. The suggestions in the Introduction, may, I hope, give some useful guidance, but neither they nor the examples are meant to be exhaustive. They never could be. Clearly, many orchestral passages would require a virtuoso performer before they could be at all adequately represented on the keyboard, and some, especially in twentieth-century works, are totally impossible. But the borderlines are not defined, and for most of us there simply remains a vast area in which we can hope to improve. For the average 'professional' music student it is a reasonable aim to be able to play with some fluency from most eighteenth and many nineteenth-century works; and, as R. O. Morris pointed out in wise words[1],

1 In the Preface to *Preparatory Exercises in Score-Reading* (R. O. Morris and Howard Ferguson).

even frustrated attempts to play elaborate scores may have a reward — in an increased ease in reading less complex ones.

I have tried to arrange the examples more or less in order of difficulty, bearing in mind that difficulty is not necessarily related to the number of staves employed. I have also tried to avoid dodging the issue by choosing only passages which lie nicely under the hands. Orchestral music is not designed to lie nicely under the hands. Even the first examples, for strings only, pose problems not normally found in conventional score-reading exercises. None of the examples has been altered or edited in any way, except for the addition of bar numbers (corresponding to the original) and the deletion of blank staves in some places. I have not tried to be consistent in the nomenclature of instruments, since it is clearly necessary that they should be recognized in more than one language.

E.T.

PLAYING
FROM AN
ORCHESTRAL SCORE

BY

ERIC TAYLOR

MUSIC DEPARTMENT
OXFORD UNIVERSITY PRESS
44 CONDUIT STREET LONDON W.1
200 MADISON AVENUE NEW YORK N.Y. 10016

ACKNOWLEDGEMENTS are due to the following for permission to use music extracts: Boosey & Hawkes Ltd. (Britten: *Four Sea Interludes —Sunday Morning*; Finzi: *Dies Natalis—Intrada*); J. & W. Chester Ltd.(Stravinsky: *L'Oiseau de Feu*; Berkeley: *Nocturne for Orchestra*); Durand & Cie (Ravel: *Shéhérazade—I. Asie.* [piano version and score]); J. Hamelle & Cie (Fauré: *Shylock—Epithalame and Nocturne*); Alfred Lengnick & Co. Ltd. (Rubbra: *Symphony No. 5 in B flat*); Novello & Co. Ltd. (Elgar: *Wand of Youth—2nd Suite, Little Bells*); Schott & Co. Ltd. (Ravel: *Pavane pour Une Infante Défunte* [piano version and score]); Oxford University Press (Vaughan Williams: *Symphony in E Minor*).

PREFACE

IT MAY be a discouraging note on which to start, but the fact has to be admitted at once that a pianist cannot do justice to a work which was conceived for the orchestra. He cannot reproduce the timbres of the different instruments. He cannot sustain notes as wind and string players can, let alone shape them with a crescendo. Much of the time he cannot even play all the notes, which no doubt is one of the reasons why composers seem to prefer to arrange their works, if at all, for two players. Indeed, it would not be much of an exaggeration to say that orchestral music is effective precisely to the extent to which it can *not* be transferred to the piano.

Nevertheless, for the purposes of study, whether for one's private benefit or as a preliminary to rehearsal, the attempt to translate an orchestral work into pianistic terms is invaluable. There are those who can 'read' a score—that is, can form a mental impression of it merely by looking at it—but they are rare, and their abilities are more likely to be the result of hard work than of a charmed birth. Moreover, a sceptic might observe that the quickest way to prove the capacity to 'read' a score is to play it. 'Reading', of course, is quite different from 'following'. With the music safely going on in the background we can all persuade ourselves that the score holds no mysteries. Real 'reading', especially as tested by playing, is not at all such an easy matter. We must then *know* whether the second horn has an F$\sharp$ or an F$\natural$, which clef the cello is in, whether the clarinets are in B$\flat$ or A. We cannot leave it to the orchestral players to work out; the record does not go on comfortably turning.

It is because playing from an orchestral score is such a help towards a detailed and accurate understanding that most degree and some diploma examinations demand it of their candidates. Yet it is not usually an easy matter, particularly in the early stages, to find a wide enough range of suitable examples to practise, especially as miniature scores are often too small to read conveniently when placed on a piano desk. It is primarily to meet this need that the present book has been compiled. The suggestions in the Introduction, may, I hope, give some useful guidance, but neither they nor the examples are meant to be exhaustive. They never could be. Clearly, many orchestral passages would require a virtuoso performer before they could be at all adequately represented on the keyboard, and some, especially in twentieth-century works, are totally impossible. But the borderlines are not defined, and for most of us there simply remains a vast area in which we can hope to improve. For the average 'professional' music student it is a reasonable aim to be able to play with some fluency from most eighteenth and many nineteenth-century works; and, as R. O. Morris pointed out in wise words[1],

---

1 In the Preface to *Preparatory Exercises in Score-Reading* (R. O. Morris and Howard Ferguson).

3

even frustrated attempts to play elaborate scores may have a reward — in an increased ease in reading less complex ones.

I have tried to arrange the examples more or less in order of difficulty, bearing in mind that difficulty is not necessarily related to the number of staves employed. I have also tried to avoid dodging the issue by choosing only passages which lie nicely under the hands. Orchestral music is not designed to lie nicely under the hands. Even the first examples, for strings only, pose problems not normally found in conventional score-reading exercises. None of the examples has been altered or edited in any way, except for the addition of bar numbers (corresponding to the original) and the deletion of blank staves in some places. I have not tried to be consistent in the nomenclature of instruments, since it is clearly necessary that they should be recognized in more than one language.

E.T.

CONTENTS

*Bar numbers have been added to show where each extract occurs in the original work.

INTRODUCTION

THE ability to play from an orchestral score is dependent on a number of other skills. The most obvious of these is the ability to read fluently in the G, C, and F clefs commonly employed in vocal and instrumental music:

Fig. 1

and the ability to play with detailed accuracy from scores for small combinations of voices or instruments which use these clefs. There are many exercises available,[1] quite apart from the amount of 'real' music published in score.[2]

The capacity to transpose easily is also required, and transposition should not be limited to the stock examination test of 'a semitone or tone up or down'. This may be all that a church organist will normally require, but an orchestral score-reader will certainly need more. He should in fact be able to transpose at least a single melodic line to any distance, though the following are especially important:

> a tone down (e.g. for Clarinets and Trumpets in B♭)
> a minor third down (e.g. for Clarinets and Trumpets in A)
> a perfect fifth down (e.g. for Horns in F, and Cor Anglais).

Other transpositions are by no means rare, however: e.g. a perfect fourth down for Horns in G, a minor or major sixth down for Horns in E or E♭, a tone or minor third *up* for Clarinets or Trumpets in D or E♭ (see Table on pp. 18-19).

Some of these transpositions present little problem if the clefs have been grasped. Transposition a tone down in the treble clef, for example, can be automatically effected by mentally substituting a tenor clef and the new key signature and transposing the result up an octave:

Fig. 2

---

1 For example: R. O. Morris and Howard Ferguson, *Preparatory Exercises in Score-Reading* (O.U.P.); C. S. Lang, *Score-Reading Exercises*, Books 1 & 2 (Novello); Aubrey Reeves, *Studies in Vocal Score-Reading*, Books 1 & 2 (Hammond); E. Beck-Slinn, *100 Graded Exercises in Vocal Score Reading* (Weekes).

2 String Quartets, for instance. The Schola Cantorum editions of *a cappella* music generally avoid adding piano reductions. Stainer & Bell in this country produce similar works, also J. & W. Chester Ltd.

Similarly:

Fig. 3

2 Trumpets in D

[Beethoven. 9th Symphony; 4th Mvt.]

sounding 8ve

The third requirement is the most difficult to define. It might be described as 'keyboard sense', though many who possess it are pretty poor performers, while on the other hand there are virtuoso pianists who lack it completely. It is the ability to play 'by ear', to extemporize, to put a workable harmony to a given tune. Some people seem almost to be born with this sense — or at least to develop it in early childhood, others to acquire it only with hard work. Nevertheless it can and must be cultivated since it is too generally important to most practical musicians to be dismissed as a fluke. Its importance at the moment lies in the fact that playing from an orchestral score almost invariably demands not only the correct reading of notes but a simultaneous 'arrangement'. Arrangement is necessary because it is usually physically impossible to play on the piano every note which appears in an orchestral score. How it can be dealt with we may consider by looking at a number of fundamental, though overlapping problems.

In the exercises listed in the footnote on p. 7 the performer is expected to play every note exactly. With an orchestral score such a literal approach is not possible, and even if it were it might well be ineffective. The aim is not to reproduce as high a percentage of notes as possible but to give the most accurate impression which can be achieved of the general sound of the score. In Example 3 (p.26), for instance, we find difficulties from bar 5 onwards. Clearly it is impossible for two hands to play all the written notes, and the usual first emergency measure of leaving out the double bass (when it is merely doubling the cello an octave lower) is no help since in bars 5 and 6 the double bass is at the same pitch as the cello. It would be possible to 'dab' at the bass notes and to catch them with the pedal,

Fig. 4

[5]

Ped _____ Ped _____

but it is a poor solution—awkward to play, dangerous as regards accuracy and, worst of all, liable to upset the flow of the quaver movement. A better solution would be to omit the violas' first quaver in bar 5, and then to put the cello up an octave:

Fig. 5

This runs into difficulties in bar 6, however, where the cellos would go above the lowest viola note and would misrepresent the harmony in the process. It would be possible to correct this by 'dabbing' the G♯ at its true pitch,

Fig. 6

but this has all the disadvantages of the first version. Moreover, the bass line is becoming distorted: note that the G♯ in bar 6 is dissonant with the F♯s in the violas and first violins (the latter being the most conspicuous). The thrust *upwards* from the D♯ adds to the tension, whereas a fall would weaken it. And we have also lost, in bar 5, the characteristic drop of a minor third which is parallel to the first violin part and which also outlines the opening of the cello melody in bar 2. Although this last detail might be improved by treating the join of bars 4-5 thus,

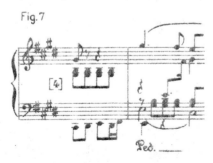

Fig. 7

the difficulties of bar 6 remain.

At this point we might do what we should have done in the first place: consider the music as a whole and see what are its characteristic features. The most obvious (from bar 5 on) are:

    (i) the melody in Violin 1

    (ii) a counter-melody in Violin 2

(iii) a bass line which, though it is largely a conventional harmonic bass, has important contours—the drop of the third in bar 5, the rise of the fourth in bar 6 and of the augmented fourth in 6-7.

That leaves us with the violas. The violas do two things: they help to provide the completeness of the harmony and the general sonority of the passage, and they maintain a background rhythm of repeated quavers. These are important features and they should certainly be added to the list as:

(iv) a sonorous and 'complete' harmony, and

(v) a repeated-quaver movement.

Neither of these features, however, is absolutely dependent on our reproducing the viola part exactly at its original pitch. The richness of harmonics which a pianist can produce with a careful use of the sustaining pedal goes a long way towards producing the required sonority. As for the quaver rhythm: it is felt chiefly as a pulsation, and as such it need not be seriously impaired if it occurs on notes other than the original ones, provided the new notes are chosen with a regard to the harmony and texture. Furthermore, the sense of quaver movement is not significantly weakened if we remove the first quaver of any group where the bass provides the necessary rhythmic pulse, i.e.:

Fig. 8

instead of

Fig. 9

With these points in mind we can achieve an arrangement which is more radical than any of our earlier versions, yet one which is reasonably playable and one which gives a fair impression of the original:

Fig. 10

Nevertheless, a lot has been lost: the little spring which the double bass pizzicato gives to the rhythm, for example, and the sustained tone of the violins which the most perfect piano cantabile cannot rival. It is interesting to compare the further problems which arise when Dvořák rescores the same passage later in the movement (Example 4, p.28). The new features which give most difficulty are: (i) the doubling of the first violin melody in octaves and (ii) the second violin figure, with its characteristic shape and its flowing semi-quaver movement. Experiment will quickly show that both of these features must be dealt with by the right hand (since the left is busy with the bass line, with the first cellos' answering phrases and so on); but it becomes equally clear that the right hand simply cannot conveniently manage both, and that some compromise is necessary. The following is a suggested solution put forward for the purpose of discussion:

Fig. 11

The second violins' semiquaver figure arose at the end of the previous passage as a linking figure. We can hardly alter its shape when the main theme re-appears (bar 54) without sacrificing the smoothness of the transition:

Fig. 12

yet to play it *and* the first violin melody in octaves is most awkward:

Fig. 13

Probably the best solution is to sacrifice the lower octave of the first violin melody, as in Fig. 11. Or we might arrange it thus:

Fig.14

At bar 58, however, the scoring changes yet again. We cannot simply repeat the lay-out which we had in bars 54-7, for this would ignore the richer texture of 58 onwards. On the other hand, if we simply shift the right hand up an octave the result will be too thin, and an un-doubled melodic line can hardly 'sing' powerfully enough in such a high register:

Fig.15

con Ped.

No: here the melody surely *needs* to be doubled at the octave. In Fig. 16, therefore, the shape of the 2nd violins' figure has been sacrificed at this point, though an attempt has been made to preserve semiquaver movement.

Fig.16

This, of course, is a real loss; but it is not so deeply felt at the join of 57-8 as it would have been at 53-4. At 53-4 the shape of the semiquaver figure was the sole linking idea. At 57-8, however, the repetition of the two-bar phrase (54-5, 56-7, 58-9) provides other connecting features: the repetition of the violin melody, of the cello answering phrases, of the harmonic progression and so on.

Another arrangement of bar 58 is given in Fig. 17,

Fig. 17

and the reader is encouraged to seek for more truthful or more comfortable versions of his own. The result, as in the examples shown, is bound to be a compromise and as such cannot be completely satisfactory; but it is in the process of achieving a reasonably effective compromise that we acquire a deeper understanding of the original orchestral music.

It is important to realise that different players may well realise the same orchestral passage differently, and yet each version may be what I have called a 'reasonably effective compromise'. There is rarely just one 'right' answer. We do things differently for a variety of reasons, though the size of our hands is one of the most important and obvious. Furthermore, in the many orchestral passages where it is clearly impossible to represent every detail there may be differing opinions, each having substance, as to what should be included and what omitted.

As an example of this we may refer to bars 11 and 12 of Example 17. The figure in descending thirds is played in three octaves (flutes, clarinets and bassoons), and, although this could be literally played by anyone whose hands were not too small, it would have to be at the expense of ignoring all the other parts completely:

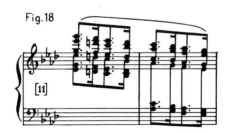

Fig. 18

Clearly this is too drastic. It would suffice to play just the clarinet parts (the bassoon parts alone would be too low and muddy, while the flute parts alone would result in too gappy a texture). Most players could also manage the first bassoon part without over-taxing the right hand:

Fig. 19

13

But this is about as much as one hand *can* manage, so that the other hand alone will have to cope with the string parts. If we transcribe these in full on to two staves, however, we shall quickly see that they cannot be encompassed by one hand, even if the double bass part is ignored:

Fig. 20

Something will have to be sacrificed, and it is at this point that there may be division of opinion. Bar 11 consists of what is fundamentally an upward curve distributed over an E♭ chord by the cellos and violas (and the 2nd violins at the end). In bar 12 the curve divides; one part (1st and 2nd violins) continuing to ascend, the other (violas and cellos) returning downwards. The whole pattern may be represented thus:—

One hand alone could manage a+b or a+c, but not both. There must be a choice between b and c. If b wins, i.e. if we regard the complete upward curve as the most important feature, we arrive at something like this as a final arrangement:

Fig. 21

If, on the other hand, c wins, i.e. if we prefer the downward curve c balancing the upward curve a, the final solution might be:

Fig. 22

In both versions there has been a good deal of pruning: not merely to make the arrangements more playable but to avoid a cumbersome texture. It is a commonplace that orchestral textures often *look* thicker than piano textures, with more doubling and more actual notes, simply because the orchestra lacks the rich source of sonority which the piano has in its sustaining pedal.

From what has been said it will be realized that one must always be prepared to work out pianistic equivalents of characteristic string and wind figurations. Ravel's arrangement of his *Shéhérazade* is an authoritative illustration of the kind of adjustments which have to be made, and the passage quoted in Ex. 26 (p. 84) is worth comparing in detail with the piano version (p. 103). Repeated notes often present a special difficulty. The techniques of double and triple tonguing in the case of wind instruments and of bowing in the case of the strings make possible the reiteration of single notes at a speed beyond the capacity of all but exceptional pianists (and pianos!). Such repetitions may be so quick that they cannot be measured rhythmically: the string bowed tremolo is a common example. Usually this can be re-arranged as a piano tremolo: bars 25-8 of Example 5, for instance, becoming

Fig. 23

In some cases it may be better to ignore a string tremolo (the viola part in Example 10 seems to be such a case): one has to admit that the piano tremolo is a poor substitute, being too heavy and thick. Nevertheless, however unsatisfactory the piano tremolo may be, it is often the only means of conveying an increase of tension and excitement. To play plain minim chords in Fig. 23 for example, would be to lose all the change of atmosphere. Similarly, rhythmically reiterated notes must normally be replaced by *some* rhythmical equivalent. In bars 196-7 of Example 14 the violins and violas are doubled by wind instruments, but we should sacrifice much of the excitement of the passage if we were to ignore the strings' semiquavers and seize instead on the quavers and crotchets in the wind parts:

Fig. 24

The following version preserves the vigour of the semiquavers:

Fig. 25

In other respects it is less literal. To preserve the clear syncopations of the woodwind the rising-scale figure in thirds has been added to the left hand—at a pitch where it does not appear in the original. This discrepancy is not in itself very important, but it entails a more serious loss in the disappearance of the repeated and dissonant E (trumpets and horns). Incidentally, the upward leap in the bass, which appears in both versions, is a distinct disadvantage.

Perhaps a word of warning should be given against misunderstanding phrasing marks in wind parts and, more especially, bowing marks in string parts. These must not be confused with piano phrasing marks though, properly understood, they are a guide to good piano phrasing. Dvořák's bowing in Example 3, for example, suggests a sostenuto line. A hiccup at the bar-lines would be inconceivable; nor, of course, is it implied by the change of bow-direction. In actual fact the passage clearly consists of overlapping phrases.

The main reason for playing from an orchestral score, let it be said again, is to deepen one's understanding of the score. To produce a satisfactory piano version of an orchestral passage is a sign that one *has* understood it. In working out one's final version, therefore, one must fully grasp all the details, even though some may have to be omitted or modified. Thus it is a good idea as a preliminary to play over the individual instruments (especially the transposing instruments!) or families—woodwind, brass, strings. (If there are two players—and two pianos—one can play the wind parts and one the strings). I have tried to avoid passages which only a very advanced pianist could hope to manage, but of course the examples will need not only working out at the keyboard but also plain practice—just as an ordinary piano piece needs practice.

Thorough practice of a large number of passages provides the best preparation for the sight-playing of orchestral scores. Nevertheless, sight-playing as such should also be attempted, if only to develop eye-speed and a quick grasp of the essentials. In sight-playing, it must be admitted, intelligent guessing often plays a part: the skill lies not so much in reading ten or fifteen

lines in a split second as in quickly spotting the most significant ones and in making the right deductions from them. Bar 16 onwards in Example 22, for instance, looks rather fearsome at a first glance; but it is not difficult to single out the flute and bassoon parts and to grasp the harmony from these alone. Even with no other information, except for the impression that the passage is fully scored, anyone with a reasonable flair for keyboard harmony would instinctively feel an equivalent lay-out on the piano, e.g.

Fig. 26

TABLE OF INSTRUMENTS

English[1]	Italian	German	French	Transposition (if any)
flute	flauto, or flauto grande	Flöte, or grosse Flöte	flûte, or grande flûte	
piccolo	flauto piccolo, or ottavino	kleine Flöte	petite flûte	2
alto flute, or bass flute, or flute in G	flauto contralto	Altflöte	flûte en sol	
oboe	oboe	Oboe, or Hoboe	hautbois	
cor anglais, or English horn	corno inglese	englisch Horn	cor anglais	
oboe d'amore	oboe d'amore	Oboe d'amore or Liebesoboe	hautbois d'amour	
clarinet in Bb	clarinetto in si bemolle	Klarinette in B	clarinette en si bémol	in Bb
in A	in la	in A	en la	in A
in Eb	in mi bemolle	in Es	en mi bémol	in Eb
in D	in re	in D	en ré	in D
bass clarinet	clarinetto basso or clarone	Bassklarinette	clarinette basse	German notation / French notation
bassoon	fagotto	Fagott	basson	
double bassoon or contrabassoon	contrafagotto	Kontrafagott	contrebasson	
horn, or French horn	corno	Horn (pl.[3]) Hörner	cor	in Bb alto
natural horn	corno naturale	Waldhorn	cor simple	
valve horn	corno ventile, or corno cromatico	Ventilhorn	cor à pistons, or cor chromatique	in A
in Bb	in si bemolle	in B	en si bémol	in Ab
in A	in la	in A	en la	in G
in Ab	in la bemolle	in As	en la bémol	
in G	in sol	in G	en sol	

English	Italian	German	French
in F	in fa	in F	en fa
in E	in mi	in E	en mi
in Eb	in mi bemolle	in Es	en mi bémol
in D	in re	in D	en ré
in C	in do	in C	en ut
trumpet	tromba (pl. trombe)	Trompete	trompette
cornet	cornetta	Kornett	cornet à pistons
trombone	trombone (pl. tromboni)	Posaune	trombone
tuba	tuba	Tuba	tuba
kettle drums	timpani	Pauken	timbales
side drum, or snare drum	tamburo piccolo, or tamburo militare	kleine Trommel	caisse claire, or tambour militaire
bass drum	cassa, or gran cassa	grosse Trommel	grosse caisse
cymbals	piatti, or cinelli	Becken	cymbales
gong	tam-tam	Tam-tam	tam-tam
triangle	triangolo	Triangel	triangle
bells	campane	Glocken	cloches
glockenspiel	campanelli	Glockenspiel	jeu de timbres, or carillon
xylophone	xilofono, or silofono	Xylophon	xylophone
harp	arpa	Harfe	harpe
violin	violino	Violine	violon
viola	viola	Bratsche	alto
cello	violoncello	Violoncell	violoncelle
double bass, or bass	contrabasso, or basso	Kontrabass	contrebasse

1. The 'English' terms given are those generally accepted in modern usage, even though they are in some cases foreign words.
2. The note in brackets is always the *written* note. It is followed by the note which is actually sounded (i.e. the 'concert' note). The key-signatures of all transposing parts must, of course, be adjusted, with one exception: horn parts are written without key-signatures at all times, with necessary accidentals added throughout. Modern composers occasionally give the horns a key-signature, but this is not the standard practice.
3. Plurals are usually clear enough, but I have given them in a few cases where they are a little less obvious or where there may be confusion: 'trombe', for example, is *not* a contraction for trombone!
4. Note that in the treble clef the horn *always* sounds lower than written: a horn in C, therefore, sounds an octave lower than written. When a horn uses the bass clef it is customarily written an octave lower than it would otherwise have been, e.g.:

Composers who do not observe this illogical convention are usually wise enough to draw attention to the fact in a footnote. (See also footnote 2).
5. Contemporary composers usually write cello parts at the pitch of their actual sounds throughout. Formerly it was the practice to write parts an octave too high where they used the treble clef, unless a passage in the tenor clef preceded the treble clef.

2

Andante molto moderato

3

26

4

28

8

8

Allegro spiritoso (♩=80)

Copyright 1945 by Boosey & Hawkes Ltd.
Reprinted by permission of Boosey & Hawkes Music Publishers Ltd.

9

38

10

Bewegt, doch nicht zu schnell

* i.e. Recorders. Notice the position of the G clef: This is the 'French violin clef' with G on the bottom line (compare the bass clef).

See page 100 for the composer's piano version of this passage.

13

* The score is written in C (i.e. as the instruments sound).

Assai moderato

53

Andante

17
Un poco allegretto e grazioso

56

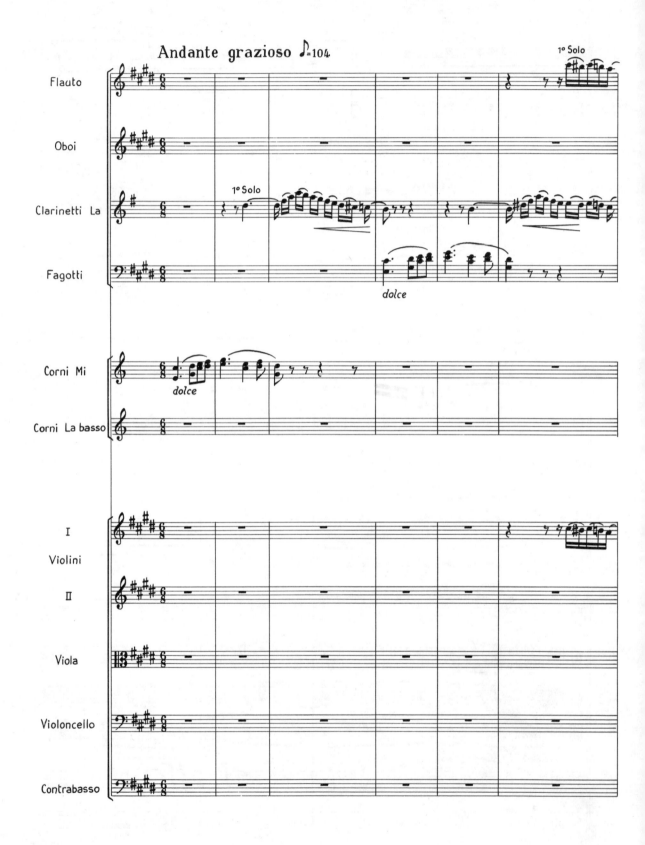

Andante cantabile, con alcuna licenza ($\bullet$.=54)

20

21

* N.B. Key-signatures.

Adagio religioso ♪= 76

See page 101 for the composer's piano version of this passage.

By permission of Editio Musica, Budapest.

* The notes in brackets are alterations written by hand in the parts owned by the Budapest Philharmonic Society, presumably by the composer himself or with his approval.

See page 102 for the composer's piano version of this passage.

26

See page 103 for the composer's piano version of this passage.

30

APPENDIX

I

By permission of Editio Musica, Budapest.

INDEX OF WORKS USED IN MUSIC EXAMPLES